INEXPLICABLE FAITH

*I know whom I have believed,
and am persuaded that he is able
to keep that which I have committed
unto him against that day.*

2 Timothy 1:12

by
Franklin N. Abazie

Inexplicable Faith
COPYRIGHT 2017 BY Franklin N Abazie
ISBN: 978-1-945-13306-0

All right reserved. This book or any portion thereof may not be reproduced or used in any manner whatsoever without the express written permission of the publisher, except for the use of brief quotations in a book review. All Bible quotes are from King James Version and others as noted.

Published by: F N ABAZIE PUBLISHING HOUSE—
aka, Empowerment Bookstore

That I may publish with the voice of thanksgiving and tell of all thy wondrous works.
Psalms 26:7

To order additional copies, wholesales or booking call:
the Church office (973-372-7518)
or Empowerment Bookstore Hotline (973-393-8518)

Worship address:
343 Sanford Avenue, Newark, New Jersey 07106
Administrative Head Office address:
33 Schley Street Newark New Jersey 07112
Email: pastorfranknto@yahoo.com
Website www.fnabaziehealingministries.org
Publishing House: www.fnabaziepublishinghouse.org

This book is a production of F N Abazie Publishing House. A publication Arms of Miracle of God Ministries 2016. First Edition

CONTENTS

THE MANDATE OF THE COMMISSION......iv
ARMS OF THE COMMISSION......................v
INTRODUCTION..vi

CHAPTER 1
How to Develop Faith In God.................24

CHAPTER 2
The Mystery of Faith Healing..................39

CHAPTER 3
The Conquering Power of Faith...............64

CHAPTER 4
Prayer of Salvation.....................................88

CHAPTER 5
About the Author.......................................99

THE MANDATE OF THE COMMISSION

"The moment is due to impact your world through the revival of the healing & miracle ministry of Jesus Christ of Nazareth.

"I am sending you to restore health unto thee and I will heal thee of thy wounds, said the Lord of Host."

ARMS OF THE COMMISSION

1) F N Abazie Ministries—Miracle of God Ministries (Miracle Chapel Intl)

2) F N Abazie TV Ministries: Global Television Ministry Outreach

3) F N Abazie Radio Ministries: Radio Broadcasting Outreach

4) F N Abazie Publishing House: Book Publication

5) F N Abazie Bible School: also called Word of Healing Bible School (W.O.H.B.S.)

6) F N Abazie Evangelistic Ass: Miracle of God Ministries: Global Crusade

7) Empowerment Bookstore: Book distribution

8) F N Abazie Helping Hands: Meeting the Help of the Needy Worldwide

9) F N Abazie Disaster Recovery Mission: Global Disaster Recovery

10) F N Abazie Prison Ministry: Prison Ministry For All Convicts "Second Chance"

Some of our ministry arms are awaiting the appointed time to commence.

INTRODUCTION

REASONS WHY WE MUST WORSHIP GOD

HE IS OUR CREATOR

1) We must worship Him because He is our creator.

2) We must worship Him because He is sovereign.

3) We must worship Him because we are made in His image.

4) We must worship Him because our worship attracts His presence.

5) We must worship Him for our faith in Him to grow.

6) We must worship Him to nourish and reactivate our spirit man.

7) We must worship Him because it activates our faith in Him.

8) We must worship Him to retain the Joy of the Lord.

9) We worship Him to evict depression, envy and malice.

10) We worship Him to be happy and to escape strife and hatred.

11) We worship Him to escape bitterness, stress, anger and misery.

BENEFITS OF OUR WORSHIP

1) Worship is medicinal—it heals our soul, body and spirit man.

2) Worship is supernatural—it positions us for constant victory in life.

3) Worship is spiritual—it grants us hope and faith in Him.

4) Worship is a mystery—it keeps us on the winning side of life.

5) Worship is faithful—it encourages us to put

up the fight.

6) Worship is strengthening—it reduces the size of our problem.

7) Worship is devotional—it proves our loyalty.

8) Worship is humbling—it proves our meekness before God.

9) Worship is power—it grants us access into signs and wonders.

10) Worship is divine—it accelerates divine intervention.

11) Worship is pleasing—God takes pleasure in it.

12) Worship is a treasure—it catches the attention of God.

13) Worship is rewarding—it brings God into our trials.

14) Worship is reciprocal—it provokes God into action.

15) Worship is glorifying, it magnifies God in our situation.

16) Worship is a blessing, it opens the flood gate of heaven.

17) Worship is our responsibility, it delivers us out of obscurity.

18) Worship is deliverance, it releases us out of captivity.

19) Worship is deeper, God looks for us to prove His divinity.

20) Worship is a reminder, God remembers His promises.

21) Worship is protection, we secure His protection.

22) Worship is unity, it grants us angelic help.

BEWARE LEST YOU FORGET

And when ye see this, your heart shall rejoice, and your bones shall flourish like an herb: and the hand of the Lord shall be known toward his servants, and his indignation toward his enemies. For, behold, the Lord will come with fire, and with his chariots like a whirlwind, to render his anger with fury, and his rebuke with flames of fire. For by fire and by his sword will the Lord plead with all flesh: and the slain of the Lord shall be many.
Isaiah 66:14-16

It is written: *"Be not deceived; God is not mocked: for whatsoever a man soweth, that shall he also reap."* (Galatians 6:7) One of the greatest advantages you have reading this page is to respect, revere and honor God in your life. Some topics in the pages of this book perhaps might not capture your interest. But let this page represent the entire book and the message.

Then beware lest thou forget the Lord, which brought thee forth out of the land of Egypt, from the house of bondage.
Deuteronomy 6:12

No matter how big and great you grow in life, never forget your God. We must acknowledge the Lord and give Him the praise in our life. Most of us live like we are invincible. We operate like we are immune to life's challenges, sickness and disease.

> *Give glory to the Lord your God,*
> *before he cause darkness,*
> *and before your feet stumble*
> *upon the dark mountains, and,*
> *while ye look for light, he turn it*
> *into the shadow of death, and make it*
> *gross darkness. But if ye will not hear it,*
> *my soul shall weep in secret places for your pride;*
> *and mine eye shall weep sore,*
> *and run down with tears,*
> *because the Lord's flock is carried away captive.*
> **Jeremiah 13:16-17**

A careful examination of these few true stories below will help us have respect for God and for the covenant. It is written— *"But seek ye first the kingdom of God, and his righteousness; and all these things shall be added unto you."* (Matthew 6:33)

John Lennon (singer with the Beatles)
About 50 years ago, during an interview with a magazine journalist, Lennon said: "Christianity will end, it will disappear. I do not have to argue about that. I am certain. Jesus was okay, but his subjects were too simple. Today we are more famous than Him." (1966) Years after claiming the Beatles were more famous than Jesus Christ, Lennon was shot six times.

Tancredo Neves (president of Brazil)
During his presidential campaign, Neves said "if [I] got 500,000 votes from [my] party, not even God would remove [me] from the presidency." Neves got the votes, but he got sick a day before his inauguration and died.

Cazuza (Bisexual Brazilian composer / singer / poet)
During a show in Canecio (Rio de Janeiro), while smoking his cigarette, Cazuza puffed out some smoke into the air and said: "God, that's for you." He'd later die at 32 of lung cancer.

The man who built the Titanic
After the construction of the Titanic cruise ship, a reporter asked the builder how safe

the ship would be. With a proud and boasting voice, he said—"Not even God can sink it." Of course, everyone knows that God eventually sank the Titanic into the ocean.

Marilyn Monroe (actress)
The spirit of the Lord led Billy Graham to visit Marilyn Monroe during a presentation of a show to minister salvation to her. After hearing what the preacher had to say, she said: "I don't need your Jesus." A week later, she was found dead in her apartment

Bon Scott (singer)
The late vocalist for the heavy metal group AC/DC. On one of his 1979 songs he sang: "Don't stop me; I'm going down all the way, down the highway to hell." On February 19, 1980, Bon Scott was found dead. He choked on his own vomit.

Campinas (2005)
In Campinas, Brazil, a group of friends having a drunken good time went to pick up a friend. The mother accompanied the friend to the car and was so worried about the drunkenness of her friends, she said to her daughter, who

was already seated in the car: "My daughter, go with God and may He protect you." She responded: "Only if He travels in the trunk, 'cause inside here it's already full." Hours later, news came that they had been involved in a fatal accident. Everyone had died. The car could not be recognized for what type of car it had been. But surprisingly, the trunk was intact. The police said there was no way the trunk could have remained intact. To their surprise, inside the trunk was a crate of eggs—none of which were broken.

Christine Hewitt
(Jamaican journalist and entertainer)

She said the Bible (Word of God) was the worst book ever written. In June 2006, she was found burned beyond recognition in her car.

These few stories are true tales anyone can investigate. We share these stories not to frighten anyone, but to instill the fear of God in your heart. *"I will send my fear before thee, and will destroy all the people to whom thou shalt come."* (Exodus 23:27)

There are many more Biblical stories to attest to my argument. We must beware of

what we say concerning God with our mouth.
"Suffer not thy mouth to cause thy flesh to sin; neither say thou before the angel, that it was an error: wherefore should God be angry at thy voice, and destroy the work of thine hands?" (Ecclesiastes 5:6)

WHAT TO DO WHEN MIRACLES SEEM TO BE DELAYED

1. Praise God, even in times of trouble, trial and tribulations.
2. Be expectant—expect God to move beyond imagination.
3) Be willing and obedient—God looks at your obedience in times of delay.
4) Be focused—God expects us to pay relevant attention to details.
5) Do not quit—if we must emerge winners, quitting is not an option.
6) Be positive—it can only get better, so be positive.
7) Be optimistic—your case is different so be optimistic in life.
8) Develop all possibilities mentality—every limitation is within your faith.

WHAT TO DO WHEN OTHERS SEEM TO GET THEIR MIRACLES

Hope in God
If God has done something to other individuals, we must celebrate with them. It is a sign that we are next in line. Whenever we celebrate with others, we are next in line for a miracle. We must hope and have faith in God. *"I have rejoiced in the way of thy testimonies, as much as in all riches."* (Pslams 119:14) God does not look like man looks. Because God searches the heart, we must therefore be glad to hear the testimonies of others. It is written: *"Thy testimonies also are my delight and my counselors."* (Psalms 119:24)

Have faith in God
Unless we develop strong faith and confidence in God, we will never experience our miracles. Often God will put us on a test. Unless we pass the faith test, we will never encounter God. *"God left him, to try him, that he might know all that was in his heart."* (2 Chronicles 32:31)

We must be focused
It is written: *"For his anger endureth but a moment; in his favour is life: weeping may endure for a night,*

but joy cometh in the morning." (Pslams 30:5) A wise man once said, "Unless we focus, we will end up like locust, and unless we fast we will not last." Every time we are distracted, we miss our miracle from God. Focus comes with dedication and discipline in life. Jesus promised that as long as we remain faithful and focused, we will never encounter the supernatural. *"And Jesus said unto him, No man, having put his hand to the plough, and looking back, is fit for the kingdom of God."* (Luke 9:62)

WHAT TO DO WHEN THINGS GET WORSE WHILE SEEKING GOD

Trust in God

It is written: *"Trust in the Lord with all thine heart; and lean not unto thine own understanding. In all thy ways acknowledge him, and he shall direct thy paths."* (Proverbs 3:5-6)

In the midst of calamity and prevailing circumstances we must trust in God.

"Although the fig tree shall not blossom, neither shall fruit be in the vines; the labour of the olive shall fail, and the fields shall yield no meat; the flock shall be cut off from the fold, and there shall be no

herd in the stalls: Yet I will rejoice in the Lord, I will joy in the God of my salvation." (Habakkuk 3:17-8)

Do not be anxious
"Do not be anxious about anything, but in every situation, by prayer and petition, with thanksgiving, present your requests to God." (Philippians 4:6)

We must develop a mindset to be at peace at all times. Although the future is uncertain, we cannot change the past. A wise man once said, "When you are depressed, you are living in the past. When you are anxious you are living in the future. But when you are at peace, you are living in the present."

God will bring a change at the appointed time

If a man die, shall he live again? all the days of my appointed time will I wait, till my change come.
Job 14:14

Even if things get bad when seeking the face of God, be determined to wait for your change. When the battle gets worse, the miracle gets better and bigger. Whenever we are seeking God, every negative change of situation is a setup for our promotion. If only we can trust and believe in God, all things will work together for us at the appointed time.

Remember…

Those who seek God are never stranded—there is always a miracle for them.

I ENCOURAGE YOU TODAY, THERE IS A WAY OUT FOR YOU. THERE IS A WAY FORWARD FOR YOU—THERE *IS* A WAY!

STRATEGIC PRAYER POINTS

And this is the confidence that we have in him, that, if we ask any thing according to his will, he heareth us.
1 John 5:14

—Holy Spirit of God, frustrate and disappoint everyone that is against my life and family, in the name of Jesus.

—Father Lord, destroy every demonic network and trap against my progress in life, in the name of Jesus.

—Fire of God, destroy every demonic projection and curse against my life and destiny, in the name of Jesus.

—Break every spell and curse pronounced

against my destiny, in the name of Jesus.

—Hand of God, cage every power militating against my rising in life, in the name of Jesus.

—Power of God, silence every voice raising a counter motion against my elevation, in the mighty name of Jesus.

—Blood of Jesus, neutralize every spirit of Balaam hired to hinder my life, ministry and career, the name of Jesus.

—Fire of God, destroy every curse that I have brought into my life through ignorance and disobedience, in the name of Jesus.

—Ancient of day, destroy every power harassing my ministry, in the name of Jesus.

—Father God, deliver me from invincible forces militating against my life and destiny.

—Power of God ,frustrate every coven and demonic network designed to frustrate and hinder my success in life, in the name of Jesus.

—I dismantle every stronghold designed to imprison my talent, in the mighty name of Jesus.

—I reject every cycle of frustration, in the name of Jesus.

—Power of God, paralyze every agent assigned to frustrate my life, in the name of Jesus.

—Finger of God, grant me supernatural speed against all my contenders, in the name of Jesus.

—By the blood of Jesus, I destroy every familiar spirit caging my life and career.
—Fire of God, arrest every demonic agent assigned to police my destiny and marriage.
—By the blood of Jesus, I proclaim no weapon fashioned against me shall ever prosper.
—Holy Spirit of God, break me through and forward in life, in the mighty name of Jesus.
—God, smash me and renew my strength, in the name of Jesus.
—Holy Spirit, open my eyes to see beyond the visible to the invisible, in the name of Jesus.
—Father Lord, grant me strength and power, in the name of Jesus
—O Lord, liberate my spirit to follow the leading of the Holy Spirit.
—Holy Spirit, teach me to pray through problems instead of praying about them, in the name of Jesus.
—Father Lord, deliver me from the false accusations in life, in the name of Jesus
—By the blood of Jesus, be roasted every evil spiritual padlock and evil chain hindering my success, in the name of Jesus.
—By the blood of Jesus, I rebuke every spirit of spiritual deafness and blindness in my life, in the name of Jesus.

—Father Lord, empower me to dominate the enemy of my destiny, in the name of Jesus.

—Jesus Christ of Nazareth, heal my infirmities, in the name of Jesus.

—Lord, anoint my eyes and my ears that they may see and hear wondrous things from heaven.

—Father Lord, anoint me with power and authority to dominate all my enemies, in the name of Jesus.

—Fire of God, roast every giant rising up against my life and career.

—Holy Spirit of God, destroy all my oppressors, in the name of Jesus.

—Angels of good news, bring my good news to me, in the mighty name of Jesus.

—Every strong man holding me down, lose your hold now, in the name of Jesus.

—I nullify every demonic prediction over my life, in the name of Jesus.

—By the blood of Jesus, I flush out every polluted deposit of the enemy in my life.

—By the blood of Jesus, I paralyze every enemy of my promotion, in the name of Jesus.

—Father Lord, destroy any power tormenting my life that is not from You.

—Holy Ghost fire, ignite the fire of revival in my life.

—By the blood of Jesus, I declare victory over every conflicting trial.

—By the blood of Jesus, I command the arrest of every demonic spirit militating against my life.

—By the blood of Jesus, I proclaim the blood of Jesus over every device of the enemy.

—By the blood of Jesus, I revoke stagnation and hardship over my life, in the name of Jesus.

—Holy Ghost fire, destroy every satanic arrangement in my life, in the name of Jesus.

CHAPTER 1

HOW TO DEVELOP FAITH IN GOD

And Jesus answering saith unto them, Have faith in God.
Mark 11:22

So many of us misinterpret and misunderstand God.

God is a spirit and God is sovereign. Unless we develop the attitude to see God as a good God and to acknowledge His doing in our lives, we limit His omnipotent power.

Cultivating an attitude of gratitude is a shortcut to develop faith in God and to encounter God in His unique dimension. Despite the prevailing challenges and obstacles that we may face on a daily basis, remaining positive and optimistic concerning any event in our life is an avenue to develop faith in God.

HOW DO I DEVELOP FAITH IN GOD?

Chapter 1   How to Develop Faith In God

Believe in God

Jesus saith unto him, Thomas, because thou hast seen me, thou hast believed: blessed are they that have not seen, and yet have believed.
John 20:29

Quite frankly, a lot of us claim we believe—but we are scared and afraid of uncertainty. We make the word of God ineffective because we are ignorant of the truth in God's word. Every time we are afraid of uncertainty, we sincerely do not believe in God. It is written: *"As soon as Jesus heard the word that was spoken, he saith unto the ruler of the synagogue, Be not afraid, only believe."*

The approved concept here is to put faith in God by believing in God—and nothing less. Often we confess that we believe in God. But when challenging circumstances arise, a lot of people fall short in life. *"Jesus saith unto her, Said I not unto thee, that, if thou wouldest believe, thou shouldest see the glory of God?"* (John 11:40)

Most pessimistic people proclaims that they believe. But when life's challenges arise, they get discouraged and faint. When the Bible said have faith in God, it is not in position to analyze the process, time and date regarding how and when God will do it. We must absolutely believe that God, in His infinite mercy, will perform and do whatsoever he promised us in life. *"Then said the Lord unto me, Thou hast well seen: for I will hasten my word to perform it."* (Jeremiah 1:12)

As thou knowest not what is the way of the spirit, nor how the bones do grow in the womb of her that is with child: even so thou knowest not the works of God who maketh all.
Ecclesiastes 11:5

HOW DO I BELIEVE IN GOD?

Every time we approve the testimonies we see and hear from others, we put ourselves in line for our own testimony. If you cannot believe what God has done for others, how can God do anything for you? *"Because they regard not the works of the Lord, nor the operation of his hands, he shall destroy them, and not build them up."* (Psalms 28:5)

Chapter 1   How to Develop Faith In God

WE MUST BELIEVE WITHOUT SEEING

Jesus saith unto him, Thomas, because thou hast seen me, thou hast believed: blessed are they that have not seen, and yet have believed.
John 20:29

We must hope in God and expect from God alone. Some of us believe, but when obstacles occur, we seek for an alternative help. *"My soul, wait thou only upon God; for my expectation is from him."* (Psalms 62:5)

WHAT DOES IT MEAN TO HAVE FAITH IN GOD?

Every time we believe in God, there must be a corresponding action to back what we are saying. Our corresponding action plan must be aligned with what God is saying in our lives. God is not a man and does not do things the same way we do things in life. As far as I know, God's promises are yea and amen. God is too faithful to fail. *"Blessed be the Lord, that hath given rest unto his people Israel, according to all that he promised: there hath not failed one word of all his good promise, which he promised by the hand of Moses his servant."* (1 Kings 8:56)

"Yea, a man may say, Thou hast faith, and I have works: shew me thy faith without thy works, and I will shew thee my faith by my works." (James 2:18)

HOW DO I DEVELOP FAITH IN GOD?

We do almost everything in life by faith involuntarily. It is written, *"For whatsoever is not of faith is sin."* (Romans 14:23) We must come to a decision point in life to accept every desired outcome as the will of God, by faith in God. To develop faith in God is to depend absolutely on God, regardless of the prevailing challenges.

Remember...

"For without faith it is impossible to please God." (Hebrew 11:6)

Now faith is the substance of things hoped for, the evidence of things not seen. For by it the elders obtained a good report. Through faith we understand that the worlds were framed by the word of God, so that things which are seen were not made of things which do appear.
Hebrew 11:1-3

"By faith we live." (Habakkuk 2:4, Romans 1:17) *"By faith ye stand."* (2 Corinthians 1:24) *"For we walk by faith."* (2 Corinthians 5:7)

Faith is absolute trust and obedience in the validity of the word of God. It is the supernatural currency for all physical transactions. We will never make a mark on Earth until we live by faith. Jesus cursed the fig tree in Mark 11:13-14 because the time of the fig tree was not yet. *"It was therefore not new to Jesus who, when Peter called into remembrance and said the fig tree which thou cursed is withered away."* (Mark 11:21) Faith in God is in our obedience and in our actions.

FAITH IS POWER

For with authority and power he commandeth the unclean spirits, and they come out.
Luke 4:36

Faith is a moving force. It takes a force for automobile to move forward or backward. We must engage into taking consequential actions in life, otherwise what we call faith is fake. Every time we develop genuine faith in

God, it generates a moving force that pushes us into taking action and making decisive decisions in life.

WHAT DO WE MEAN BY "FAITH IN GOD?"

Some weak believers claim to have faith in God, but when trouble comes they become weary and faint. A few Bible characters who stayed strong in God during times of trial will help support what we mean by faith in God.

Apostle Paul had faith in God. *"Of the Jews five times received I forty stripes save one. Thrice was I beaten with rods, once was I stoned, thrice I suffered shipwreck, a night and a day I have been in the deep; in journeyings often, in perils of waters, in perils of robbers, in perils by mine own countrymen, in perils by the heathen, in perils in the city, in perils in the wilderness, in perils in the sea, in perils among false brethren; In weariness and painfulness, in watchings often, in hunger and thirst, in fastings often, in cold and nakedness."* (2 Corinthians 11:24-27

Despite the harassment, the beating and the stoning, Apostle Paul never for once gave up on God. Apostle Paul believed in

God. *"For I know whom I have believed, and am persuaded that he is able to keep that which I have committed unto him against that day."* (2 Timothy 1:12) We must have faith in God if we are to see the manifestations of the miracles of God upon our lives. We must make up our mind to confront and withstand any opposition, challenge trials and obstacles that will come our way in our lifetime.

This includes taking the appropriate positive steps and making the right decision at the right time. What we all call "faith" is not faith unless we back our voice with an action in life. *"Yea, a man may say, Thou hast faith, and I have works: shew me thy faith without thy works, and I will shew thee my faith by my works."* (James 2:18)

FAITH IS A DEFENSE

Above all, taking the shield of faith, wherewith ye shall be able to quench all the fiery darts of the wicked.
Ephesians 6:16

Although faith in God is a shield, it also builds our system up in Christ. Everyone of faith who travails in prayers must prevail in life. The good news about faith is that it lifts our spirit and grants us the privilege of optimism even in the midst of prevailing challenging circumstances.

FAITH GRANTS REST

For whatsoever is born of God overcometh the world: and this is the victory that overcometh the world, even our faith.
1 John 5:4

We do not have a chance to prevail against any life challenges and obstacles, unless FAITH takes its perspective in our lives. FAITH is our VICTORY CERTIFICATION against all the brutal attacks of the devil. It is the mystery of faith that will subdue and overcome the wicked one (the devil).

WE WALK IN LIFE BY FAITH

For we walk by faith, not by sight.
2 Corinthians 5:7

Unless we make up our mind to live by faith, what we call faith genuinely is not faith unless there is an inner conviction of our spirit man.

WE STAND BY FAITH

Not for that we have dominion over your faith, but are helpers of: your joy: for by faith ye stand.
2 Corinthians 1:24

It takes faith to defeat oppositions. *"Wherefore take unto you the whole armour of God that ye may be able to withstand in the evil day, and having done all, to stand. Stand therefore, having your loins girt about with truth, and having on the breastplate of righteousness."*

WHAT IS INEXPLICABLE FAITH?

This is the faith that manifests with a culmination of undeniable testimonies. Maybe calling it "faith with testimony in return" is a better way to describe it. Inexplicable faith is the faith that cannot be seen, yet cannot be denied. This is the faith that generates overwhelming testimonies in someone's life, yet cannot be defined nor explained.

This faith results in unseen victory, promotion, breakthroughs and success in the midst of great impossibilities. The innumerable harvest of this faith is uncountable and undeniable, yet it cannot be ascribed, defined nor interpreted. Inexplicable faith is the application faith. This is the faith that convicts anyone who dares to believe to take genuine, qualitative action towards actualizing a well-defined goal. Or accomplishing an agenda or a mission.

We are told, *"Now faith is the substance of things hoped for, the evidence of things not seen."* Often we take the face value of this scriptural definition without putting it into practice in our lives.

HOW DOES FAITH COME?

It is written, *"So then faith cometh by hearing, and hearing by the word of God."* (Romans 10:17)

HOW DOES FAITH WORK?

It is written, *"But faith which worketh by love."*

Remember....

"Yea, a man may say, Thou hast faith, and I have works: shew me thy faith without thy works,

and I will shew thee my faith by my works."

KEYS TO PERSONAL DEVELOPMENT

Self-development is a personal decision that demands the sacrifice of determination, discipline, dedication and personal efforts. For all who desire to make an impact in their lifetime, we must embrace the character required for success. Zig Ziglar once said that "Every dummy can succeed if he or she cares to know what it takes to succeed in life."

The life of Sundays William Ashley is a prime example of men who turned their career around by self-development in life. Sundays William "Billy" Sunday (November 19, 1862 – November 6, 1935) was an American athlete who, after being a popular outfielder in baseball's National League during the 1880s, became the most celebrated and influential American evangelist during the first two decades of the 20th century. Born into poverty in Iowa, Sunday spent some years at the Iowa Soldiers' Orphans' Home before working at odd jobs and playing for local running and baseball teams. His speed and agility provided him the opportunity to play baseball in the major leagues for eight years, where he was an average hitter and a good fielder known for his baserunning.

Converting to evangelical Christianity in the 1880s, Sunday left baseball for the Christian ministry. He gradually developed his skills as a pulpit evangelist in the Midwest. During the early 20th century, he became the nation's most famous evangelist, thanks to his colloquial sermons and frenetic delivery. *"And this is the confidence that we have in him, that, if we ask any thing according to his will, he heareth us."* (1 John 5:14)

While the earth remaineth, seedtime and harvest, and cold and heat, and summer and winter, and day and night shall not cease.
Genesis 8:22

In my opinion, "input determines output." One of the greatest advantages we have in life is the free gift of time. Whatever we do with our God-given time matters most to God. To develop personally, we must utilize our time wisely. We must develop by reading, searching and improving in the area and career God has called us to in life. *"Seest thou a man diligent in his business? he shall stand before kings; he shall not stand before mean men."* (Proverbs 22:29)

We must cultivate the habit of improving our life by exercising our minds. We must become dedicated students and improve in learning and searching for new innovative ways to improve and update our lives and careers.

We must be eager to search for knowledge by reading relevant books, listening to tapes and devouring materials that challenge our minds and help build our wisdom. To develop our mind, we must be a great reader and researchers of the truth of God's word. Going to school gives us information, but prayer and meditation grants us revelation and interpretation of the truth to confront prevailing challenges in life.

Let's briefly examine a few great men who improved their lives and made an impact in their lifetime.

Benjamin Franklin

With only two years of education, Franklin dropped out of school at the age of ten, because there was no money to continue. He taught himself how to read and write. This is the same man who later invented the Franklin stone (the bi-focal lens) and lightning rod, while also being one of the founding fathers of America. And he started a university—the University of Pennsylvania.

Richard Branson

The founder of the Virgin Atlantic Airlines—a multimillion company—started as a newspaper vendor and developed a habit of reading. He once read a little book that inspired him called *Small Is Beautiful* and now he has an airline and a group of successful companies—all due largely to his commitment to personal development.

We must invest our time and resources in personal training and development. If all you have been working for you is merely what you learned in school, you'll soon be outdated. Develop yourself to the point where you become so creative, your products become outstanding and unique and can't be found anywhere else.

Greatness remains a dream until you develop yourself. Stardom is impossible until you develop yourself.

CHAPTER 2

THE MYSTERY OF FAITH HEALING

And the prayer of faith shall save the sick, and the Lord shall raise him up; and if he have committed sins, they shall be forgiven him.
James 5:15

The above scripture says, "And the prayer of faith shall save the sick." This is a mystery that the medical community has not been able to comprehend. Isn't it fascinating to medical science how faith heals the sick? We cannot understand faith healing in the energy of the flesh. What the secular world calls faith is not faith unless we operate in God. *"He made known his ways unto Moses, his acts unto the children of Israel."* (Psalms 103:7)

FAITH HEALING IS A KINGDOM MYSTERY

And he said unto him, Arise, go thy way: thy faith hath made thee whole.
Luke 17:19

*And he [Jesus] said unto her, Daughter,
be of good comfort: thy faith hath
made thee whole; go in peace.*
Luke 8:48

The above scripture says, "thy faith hath made thee whole," Over the years, the medical community has always argued and disputed the healing faith. Contrary to this prevailed argument about faith healing, the medical community has accepted faith healing as a way to cure some outstanding incurable diseases. I encourage you, whatever may be the prevailed hindrances, have faith in God and you shall overcome it in Jesus's Name. *"For whatsoever is born of God overcometh the world: and this is the victory that overcometh the world, even our faith."* (1 John 5:4)

Jesus saith unto him, Thomas, because thou hast seen me, thou hast believed: blessed are they that have not seen, and yet have believed. John **20:29**

For the most part, we focus exclusively on faith healing mystery, forgetting that we must also BELIEVE IN GOD. Faith in God is the primary link to healing. Scriptures proved that Jesus couldn't do any mighty work because he marveled at their unbelief. *"And he could there do no mighty work, save that he laid his hands upon a few sick folk, and healed them. And he marvelled because of their unbelief. And he went round about the villages, teaching."* (Mark 6:5-6)

Unbelief in God is a stumbling hindrance that will hinder the flow of healing into our lives. It takes our faith in God to initiate our desired healing from God.

Although our faith in God initiates our desired healing, the mystery of healing depends solely on God—the mighty physician. It is inevitable for the Almighty to withhold our healing in time of need, because healing is his children's bread. Remember, healing is the will of God. It is written, *"Beloved, I wish above all things that thou mayest prosper and be in health, even as thy soul prospereth."* (3 John1:2)

Our faith in God moves Him to save us. *"For by grace are ye saved through faith; and that not of yourselves: it is the gift of God."* (Ephesians 2:8) Salvation means deliverance from sins and destruction of the devil. Inside of salvation includes our healing—which is the will of God.

That it might be fulfilled, which was spoken by Isaiah the prophet, saying: "He Himself took our infirmities and bore our sicknesses." (Matthew 8:17, Isaiah 53:4-6)

HINDRANCES TO THE HEALING FAITH

Doubt

It is written: *"A double minded man is unstable in all his ways."* (James 1:8) Every time we are in doubt, we hinder the stretched arm of the Lord to heal us. If we must be healed from sickness and diseases, we must cast out all doubt and fear in the mighty name of Jesus.

Unbelief

It is written: *"And he could there do no mighty work, save that he laid his hands upon a few sick folk, and healed them. And he marvelled because of their unbelief. And he went round about the villages, teaching."* (Mark 6:5-6) Unbelief is one of the strong hindrance to healing that it can even affect the faith healer.

Fear

It is written: "For God hath not given us

the spirit of fear; but of power, and of love, and of a sound mind."2timothy1:8. God heals us with our faith, while the devil tortures and attacks us with sickness by instilling fear in our heart. *"There is no fear in love; but perfect love casteth out fear: because fear hath torment. He that feareth is not made perfect in love."* (1 John4:18)

Remember...

"For ye have not received the spirit of bondage again to fear; but ye have received the Spirit of adoption, whereby we cry, Abba, Father." (Romans 8:15)

Dishonors the faith healer

It is written: *"Be it far from me; for them that honour me I will honour, and they that despise me shall be lightly esteemed."* (1 Samuel 2:30) We must honor God's agents of healing—the prophet.

"Therefore whoever confesses Me before men, him I will also confess before My Father who is in heaven. But whoever denies Me before men, him I will also deny before My Father who is in heaven." (Matthew 10:32-33) For God to pay attention concerning our desired healing, we must honor His prophets sent our way. Most of God's

prophets who are also faith healers carry the mantle of healing concerning our lives. We must que and key into it if we are to experience God's dynamic healing mystery.

CONCLUSION OF CHAPTER 2

Healing is a mystery that works with our faith in God. But faith cannot work unless there is love in place. It is written, *"But faith which worketh by love."* (Galatians 5:6)

Remember...

"And we have known and believed the love that God hath to us. God is love; and he that dwelleth in love dwelleth in God, and God in him." (1 John 4:16)

We must prove our love for God by our service to others and to His kingdom. We must accept the free gift of salvation for the redemption of our soul. We must embrace spirituality if we are to make an impact and prosper in our lifetime.

WHAT IS THE MYSTERY OF FAITH?

Chapter 2   The Mystery of Faith Healing

And this is the confidence that we have in him, that, if we ask any thing according to his will, he heareth us.
1 John 5:14

"*Who against hope believed in hope, that he might become the father of many nations, according to that which was spoken, So shall thy seed be. And being not weak in faith, he considered not his own body now dead, when he was about an hundred years old, neither yet the deadness of Sarah's womb: He staggered not at the promise of God through unbelief; but was strong in faith, giving glory to God; And being fully persuaded that, what he had promised, he was able also to perform.*" (Romans 4:18-22)

INEXPLICABLE FAITH PRAYER POINTS

—I cancel my name and that of my family's from the death register, with the fire of God, in the mighty name of Jesus.

—Every weapon of destruction fashioned against me and my family be destroyed by the fire of God, in the name of Jesus.

—Power of God, fight for me in every area of my life, in the name of Jesus.

—Every hindrance to my breakthrough be melted by the fire of God, in the name of Jesus.

—Every evil power against me be scattered by the thunder fire of God, in the name of Jesus.

—Father Lord, destroy every evil man/woman, in the name of Jesus.

—Every failure of the past be converted to success, in Jesus' name.

—Father Lord, let the former rain, the latter rain and Your blessing pour down on me now.

—Father Lord, let all the failure turn into success for me, in the name of Jesus.

—I receive power from on high and I paralyze all the powers of darkness that are diverting my blessings, in the name of Jesus.

—Beginning from this day, I employ the services of the angels of God to open unto me

Chapter 2   The Mystery of Faith Healing

every door of opportunity and breakthroughs, in the name of Jesus.

—I will not go around in circles again, I will make progress, in the name of Jesus.

—I shall not build for another to inhabit and I shall not plant for another to eat, in the name of Jesus.

—I paralyse the powers of the emptier concerning my handiwork, in the name of Jesus.

—O Lord, let every locust, caterpillar and palmer-worm assigned to eat the fruit of my labour be roasted by the fire of God.

—The enemy shall not spoil my testimony in this programme, in the name of Jesus.

—By the blood of Jesus, I reject every backward journey, in the name of Jesus.

—By the blood of Jesus, I paralyze every strongman attached to any area of my life, in the name of Jesus.

—I pray, let every agent of shame fashioned to work against my life be paralyzed, in the name of Jesus.

—I paralyse the activities of household wickedness over my life, in the name of Jesus.

—I quench every strange fire emanating from evil tongues against me, in the name of Jesus.

—Father Lord, give me power for maximum

achievement, in the name of Jesus.

—Heavenly Father, give me comforting authority to achieve my goal.

—Blood of Jesus Christ, defend and fortify me with Your power.

—I paralyse every spirit of disobedience in my life, in Jesus' name.

—I refuse to disobey the voice of God, in the name of Jesus.

—Every root of rebellion in my life be uprooted, in Jesus' name.

—By the blood of Jesus, I destroy every witchcraft spirit in my life, in the name of Jesus.

—Perish every contradicting force promoting hindrance in my life, in Jesus' name.

—Every inspiration of witchcraft in my family, be destroyed, in the name of Jesus.

—Blood of Jesus, blot out every evil mark of witchcraft in my life, in the name of Jesus.

—Every garment put upon me by witchcraft, be torn to pieces, in the name of Jesus.

—Angels of God, begin to pursue my household enemies, let their ways be dark and slippery, in the name of Jesus.

—Lord, confuse them and turn them against themselves, in the name of Jesus.

—By the blood of Jesus, I break every evil un-

Chapter 2 The Mystery of Faith Healing

conscious agreement with household enemies concerning my miracles, in the name of Jesus.

—Household witchcraft, fall down and die, in the name of Jesus.

—Father Lord, drag all the household wickedness to the Dead Sea and bury them there.

—Father Lord, I refuse to follow the evil pattern of remote control, my household enemies.

—My life, jump out from the cage of household wickedness, in the name of Jesus.

—I command all my blessings and potentials buried by wicked household enemies to be exhumed, in the name of Jesus.

—I will see the goodness of the Lord in the land of the living, in the name of Jesus.

—Everything done against me to spoil my joy receive destruction, in the name of Jesus.

—Father Lord, as Abraham received favour in Your eyes, let me receive Your favour, so that I can excel in every area of my life.

—Lord Jesus, help my shortcomings and infirmities, in the name of Jesus.

—It does not matter whether I deserve it or not, I receive immeasurable favour from the Lord, in the name of Jesus.

—By the blood of Jesus I receive every blessing God has apportioned to me, in the name of Jesus.

—My blessing will not be transferred to my neighbor, in the name of Jesus.

—Father Lord, disgrace every power that is tormenting my breakthrough, in the name of Jesus.

—Every step I take shall lead to outstanding success, in Jesus' name.

—I shall prevail with man and with God in every area of my life, in the name of Jesus.

—Break to pieces every habitation of infirmity in my life, in the name of Jesus.

—My body, soul and spirit, reject every evil load, in Jesus' name.

—Evil foundation in my life, I pull you down today, in the mighty name of Jesus.

—Every inherited sickness in my life, depart from me now, in the name of Jesus.

—Every evil water in my body, get out, in the name of Jesus.

—By the blood of Jesus, I cancel the effect of every evil dedication in my life, in the name of Jesus.

—Holy Ghost fire, immunize my blood against satanic poisoning, in the name of Jesus.

—Father Lord, put self-control in my mouth, in the name of Jesus.

Chapter 2 The Mystery of Faith Healing

—I refuse to get accustomed to sickness, in the name of Jesus.

—Every door open to infirmity in my life, be permanently closed today, in the name of Jesus.

—Every power contenting with God in my life, be roasted, in the name of Jesus.

—Every power preventing God's glory from manifesting in my life, be paralysed, in the name of Jesus.

—I loose myself from the spirit of desolation, in the name of Jesus.

—Father Lord, break me through in my home, in the name of Jesus.

—Father Lord keep in me healthy, in the name of Jesus.

—Father Lord break me through in my business, in the name of Jesus.

—Let God be God in my economy, in the name of Jesus.

—Glory of God, envelope every department of my life, in the name of Jesus.

—The Lord that answereth by fire, be my God, in the name of Jesus.

—By the blood of Jesus, all my enemies shall scatter to rise no more, in the name of Jesus.

—Blood of Jesus, cry against all evil gatherings

arranged for my sake, in the name of Jesus.

—Father Lord, convert all my past failures to unlimited victories, in the name of Jesus.

—Lord Jesus, create room for my advancement in every area of my life.

—All evil thoughts against me, Lord turn them to be good for me.

—Father Lord, give evil men for my life where evil decisions have been taken against me, in the name of Jesus.

—Father Lord, advertise Your dumbfounding prosperity in my life.

—Let the showers of dumbfounding prosperity fall in every department of my life, in the name of Jesus.

—By the blood of Jesus, I claim all my prosperity in the name of Jesus.

—Every door of my prosperity that has been shut, be opened now, in the name of Jesus.

—Father Lord, convert my poverty to prosperity, in the name of Jesus.

—Father Lord, convert my mistake to perfection, in the name of Jesus.

—Father Lord, convert my frustration to fulfillment, in the name of Jesus.

—Father Lord, bring honey out of the rock for me, in the name of Jesus.

Chapter 2 The Mystery of Faith Healing

—By the blood of Jesus, I stand against every evil covenant of sudden death, in the name of Jesus.

—By the blood of Jesus, I break every conscious and unconscious evil covenant of untimely death, in the name of Jesus.

—You spirit of death and hell, you have no document in my life, in the name of Jesus.

—You stones of death, depart from my ways, in the name of Jesus.

—Father Lord, make me a voice of deliverance and blessing.

—By the blood of Jesus, I tread upon the high places of the enemies, in the name of Jesus.

—I bind and render useless, every blood-sucking demon, in the name of Jesus.

—You evil current of death, lose your grip over my life, in the name of Jesus.

—By the blood of Jesus, I frustrate the decisions of the evil openers in my family, in the name of Jesus.

—Fire of protection, cover my family, in the name of Jesus.

—Father Lord, make my way perfect, in the name of Jesus.

—Throughout the days of my life, I shall not be put to shame, in the name of Jesus.

—By the blood of Jesus, I reject every garment of shame, in the name of Jesus.

—By the blood of Jesus, I reject every shoe of shame, in the name of Jesus.

—By the blood of Jesus, I reject every head-gear and cap of shame, in the name of Jesus.

—Shamefulness shall not be my lot, in the mighty name of Jesus.

—Be removed every demonic limitation of my progress as a result of shame, in the name of Jesus.

—Every network of shame around me be paralysed, in the name of Jesus.

—Those who seek for my shame shall die for my sake, in the name of Jesus.

—As far as shame is concerned, I shall not record any point for satan, in the name of Jesus.

—In the name of Jesus, I shall not eat the bread of sorrow, I shall not eat the bread of shame and I shall not eat the bread of defeat.

—No evil will touch me throughout my life, in the name of Jesus.

—By the blood of Jesus, in every area of my life, my enemies will not catch me, in the name of Jesus.

—By the blood of Jesus, in every area of my life, I shall run and not grow weary, I shall walk

Chapter 2 The Mystery of Faith Healing

and shall not faint.

—Father Lord, in every area of my life, let not my life disgrace You.

—By the blood of Jesus, I will not be a victim of failure and I shall not bite my finger for any reason, in the name of Jesus.

—Holy Spirit of God, help me O Lord, to meet up with God's standard for my life.

—By the blood of Jesus, I refuse to be a candidate to the spirit of amputation, in the name of Jesus.

—By the blood of Jesus, with each day of my life, I shall move to higher ground, in the name of Jesus.

—Every spirit of shame set in motion against my life, I bind you, in the name of Jesus.

—Every spirit competing with my breakthroughs, be chained, in the name of Jesus.

—By the blood of Jesus, I bind every spirit of slavery, in the name of Jesus.

—By the blood of Jesus, in every day of my life, I disgrace all my stubborn pursuers, in the name of Jesus.

—By the blood of Jesus, I bind every spirit of Herod, in the name of Jesus.

—Every spirit challenging my God, be disgraced, in Jesus' name.

—Every Red Sea before me, be parted, in the name of Jesus.
—By the blood of Jesus, I command every spirit of bad-ending to be bound in every area of my life, in the name of Jesus.
—By the blood of Jesus, every spirit of Saul be disgraced in my life, in the name of Jesus.
—By the blood of Jesus, every spirit of Pharaoh be disgraced in my life, in Jesus' name.
—By the blood of Jesus, I reject every evil invitation to backwardness, in Jesus' name.
—By the blood of Jesus, I command every stone of hindrance in my life to be rolled away, in the name of Jesus.
—Father Lord, roll away every stone of poverty from my life, in the name Jesus.
—Let every stone of infertility in my marriage be rolled away, in the name of Jesus.
—Let every stone of non-achievement in my life be rolled away, in the name of Jesus.
—My God, roll away every stone of hardship and slavery from my life, in the name of Jesus.
—My God, roll away every stone of failure planted in my life, in my home and in my business, in the name of Jesus.
—You stones of hindrance planted at the edge of my breakthroughs, be rolled away, in the

Chapter 2 The Mystery of Faith Healing

name of Jesus.

—You stones of stagnancy stationed at the border of my life, be rolled away, in the name of Jesus.

—My God, let every stone of the 'amputator' planted at the beginning of my life, at the middle of my life and at the end of my life, be rolled away, in the name of Jesus.

—Father Lord, I thank You for all the stones You have rolled away, I forbid their return, in the name of Jesus.

—Let the power from above come upon me, in the name of Jesus.

—Father Lord, advertise Your power in every area of my life, in the name of Jesus.

—Father Lord, make me a power generator throughout the days of my life, in the name of Jesus.

—Let the power to live a holy life throughout the days of my life fall upon me, in the name of Jesus.

—Let the power to live a victorious life throughout the days of my life fall upon me, in the name of Jesus.

—Let the power to prosper throughout the days of my life fall upon me, in the name of Jesus.

—Let the power to be in good health throughout the days of my life fall upon me, in the name of Jesus.

—Let the power to disgrace my enemies throughout the days of my life fall upon me, in the name of Jesus.

—Let the power of Christ rest upon me now, in the name of Jesus.

—Let the power to bind and loosen fall upon me now, in the name of Jesus.

—Father Lord, let Your key of revival unlock every department of my life for Your revival fire, in the name of Jesus.

—Every area of my life that is at the point of death, receive the touch of revival, in the name of Jesus.

—Father Lord, send down Your fire and anointing into my life, in the name of Jesus.

—Every uncrucified area in my life, receive the touch of fire and be crucified, in the name of Jesus.

—Let the fire fall and consume all hindrances to my advancement, in the name of Jesus.

—You stubborn problems in my life, receive the Holy Ghost dynamite, in the name of Jesus.

—You carryover miracle from my past receive the touch of fire, in the name of Jesus.

—Holy Ghost fire, baptize me with prayer mir-

Chapter 2   The Mystery of Faith Healing

acle, in Jesus' name.
—By the blood of Jesus, every area of my life that needs deliverance, receive the touch of fire and be delivered, in the name of Jesus.
—Let my angels of blessing locate me now, in the name of Jesus.
—Every satanic programme of impossibility, I cancel you now, in the name of Jesus.
—Every household wickedness and its programme of impossibility, be paralysed, in the name of Jesus.
—No curse will land on my head, in the name of Jesus.
—Throughout the days of my life, I will not waste money on my health: the Lord shall be my healer, in the name of Jesus.
—Throughout the days of my life, I will be in the right place at the right time.
—Throughout the days of my life, I will not depart from the fire of God's protection, in the name of Jesus.
—Throughout the days of my life, I will not be a candidate for incurable disease, in the name of Jesus.
—Every weapon of captivity be disgraced, in the name of Jesus.
—Lord, before I finish this programme, I need

an outstanding miracle in every area of my life.

—Let every attack planned against the progress of my life be frustrated, in the name of Jesus.

—I command the spirits of harassment and torment to leave me, in the name of Jesus.

—Lord, begin to speak soundness into my mind and being, in Jesus' name.

—I reverse every witchcraft curse issued against my progress, in the name of Jesus.

—I condemn all the spirits condemning me, in the name of Jesus.

—Let divine accuracy come into my life and operations, in the name of Jesus.

—No evil directive will manifest in my life, in the name of Jesus.

—Let the plans and purposes of heaven be fulfilled in my life, in the name of Jesus.

—O Lord, bring to me friends that reverence Your name and keep all others away.

—Let divine strength come into my life, in the name of Jesus.

—Let every stronghold working against my peace be destroyed, in the name of Jesus.

—Let the power to destroy every decree of darkness operating in my life fall upon me now, in the mighty name of Jesus.

—Lord, deliver my tongue from evil silence.

Chapter 2 The Mystery of Faith Healing

—Lord, let my tongue tell others of Your life.

—Lord, loosen my tongue and use it for Your glory.

—Lord, let my tongue bring straying sheep back to the fold.

—Lord, let my tongue strengthen those who are discouraged.

—Lord, let my tongue guide the sad and the lonely.

—Lord, baptise my tongue with love and fire.

—Let every unrepentant and stubborn pursuers be disgraced in my life, in the name of Jesus.

—Let every iron-like curse working against my life be broken by the blood of Jesus, in the name of Jesus.

—Let every problem designed to disgrace me receive open shame, in the name of Jesus.

—Let every problem anchor in my life be uprooted, in Jesus' name.

—Multiple evil covenants, be broken by the blood of Jesus, in the name of Jesus.

—Multiple curses, be broken by the blood of Jesus, in —Jesus' name.

—Everything done against me with evil padlocks, be nullified by the blood of Jesus, in the name of Jesus.

—Everything done against me at any crossroads, be nullified by the blood of Jesus, in the name of Jesus.

—Let every stubborn and prayer resisting demon receive stones of fire and thunder, in the name of Jesus.

—Every stubborn and prayer-resisting sickness, lose your evil hold upon my life, in the name of Jesus.

—Every problem associated with the dead, be smashed by the blood of Jesus, in the name of Jesus.

—I recover my stolen property sevenfold, in the name of Jesus.

—Let every evil memory about me be erased by the blood of Jesus, in the name of Jesus.

—By the blood of Jesus, I disallow my breakthroughs from being caged, in Jesus' name.

—Let the sun of my prosperity arise and scatter every cloud of poverty, in the name of Jesus.

—I decree unstoppable advancement upon my life, in Jesus' name.

—I soak every day of my life in the blood of Jesus and in signs and wonders, in the name of Jesus.

—I break every stronghold of oppression in my life, in Jesus' name.

—Let every satanic joy about my life be terminated, in the name of Jesus.

—I paralyse every household wickedness, in the name of Jesus.

—Let every satanic spreading river dry up by the blood of Jesus, in the name of Jesus.

—I bind every ancestral spirit and command them to loose their hold over my life, in the name of Jesus.

CHAPTER 3

THE CONQUERING POWER OF FAITH

Nay, in all these things we are more than conquerors through him that loved us.
Romans 8:37

For whatsoever is born of God overcometh the world: and this is the victory that overcometh the world, even our faith.
1 John 5:4

The above scripture says, "for whatsoever is born of God." That statement is powerful scripture. The verse states that faith is the vehicle for us to conquer and dominate in life. Faith in God is the catalyst-this I mean faith in God's word is all we need to activate the promises of God. By this, we mean faith in God's word to confront all challenges, hindrances and obstacles of life. *"But without faith it is impossible to please him."* (Hebrews 11:6)

"Nay, in all these things we are more than conquerors through him that loved us." (Romans 8:37)

Chapter 3   The Conquering Power of Healing

WHAT IS THE CONQUERING POWER OF FAITH?

The conquering faith is born out of our mental conviction about the finished work of Jesus Christ. This faith is the inner conviction of things not seen, yet we believe in God's word. About father Abraham, the Bible says: *"And he believed in the Lord; and he counted it to him for righteousness."* (Genesis 15:6)

The conquering power of faith can best be understood in the supernatural realm. As a natural man, it is difficult for every man from the flesh to understand the conquering force of faith. It takes an inner spirit conviction in the things that we do not see, feel touch, smell and taste for us to be in command in the supernatural.

We must embrace the application of faith in our lives with caution and love, reverence and fear of God. Unless we are open-minded, we will miss the mysteries about faith in God. Every one of us applies faith to our everyday life. *"Now faith is the substance of things hoped for, the evidence of things not seen."* (Hebrews 11:1)

Faith is evidence that God's word is true. This includes making God's word a law and final in our lives. It includes making God's will my will and the realization that God's plan is my pattern. His way is my way, henceforth with me—that is, we're making God's word to have the final say in our lives. *"For I know whom I have believed, and am persuaded that he is able to keep that which I have committed unto him against that day."* (2 Timothy 1:12)

"While we look not at the things which are seen, but at the things which are not seen: for the things which are seen are temporal; but the things which are not seen are eternal." (2 Corinthians 4:18)

Our root in Christ Jesus, as the seed of Abraham, must be evident in our lives. *"And if ye be Christ's, then are ye Abraham's seed, and heirs according to the promise."* (Galatians 3:29)

WHAT DID ABRAHAM DO?

"Who against hope believed in hope, that he might become the father of many nations, according to that which was spoken, So shall thy seed be. And being not weak in faith, he considered not his own body now dead, when he was about an hundred years old, neither yet the deadness of Sarah's womb: He staggered not at the promise of God through un-

belief; but was strong in faith, giving glory to God; And being fully persuaded that, what he had promised, he was able also to perform." (Romans 4:18-21)

WHAT ELSE DID ABRAHAM DO?

*Now the Lord had said unto Abram,
Get thee out of thy country,
and from thy kindred, and from
thy father's house, unto a land that
I will shew thee: And I will make of thee
a great nation, and I will bless thee,
and make thy name great; and thou shalt
be a blessing: And I will bless them that
bless thee, and curse him that curseth thee:
and in thee shall all families of the earth
be blessed. So Abram departed,
as the Lord had spoken unto him;
and Lot went with him: and Abram
was seventy and five years old
when he departed out of Haran.*
Genesis 12:1-4

Contrary to what we see and believe, the conquering faith is the decisive faith. This faith operates in us taking action concerning our lives and future. Every faith without action is dead. The scripture says, *"as the body without the spirit is dead,"* so faith without works is dead also. This work, in my own understanding, is in taking action in life. As long as we have our mind on Christ Jesus, we must be action-oriented and focused in life.

"I am crucified with Christ: nevertheless I live; yet not I, but Christ liveth in me: and the life which I now live in the flesh I live by the faith of the Son of God, who loved me, and gave himself for me." (Galatians 2:20)

The conquering faith is the living force pushing us into concrete action that will determine our future. We often think that faith is the key to getting something from God. However, this is backwards. Faith is actually the evidence that God has gotten something in stock for us. If we must access His riches in stock, we must prove it by our evidence. And the evidence is in moving. It is written of Noah: *"By faith Noah, being warned of God of things not seen as yet, moved with fear."* (Hebrews 11:7)

THE WINNING SECRET TO SUCCESS IN LIFE

Skill is the ability to do something well in life. This includes intensive learning and studying without limit. Skill has to do with techniques and the know-how we manifest in our careers. This includes apprenticeship, intellectual wisdom, secular knowledge, innovative strategies and techniques and approachs to meet complex life and business demands.

The Bible says, *"Do you know a man who is skilled? He will serve before kings, and he will not serve men."* (NIV) Oprah Winfrey once said; *"Excellence is the greatest deterrent to racism and sectarianism."* Unless we develop ourselves to be outstanding in life, we will never stand out in our area of calling.

HOW TO PROVOKE DIVINE INTERVENTION

BE BORN AGAIN

"Jesus answered and said unto him, Verily, verily, I say unto thee, Except a man be born again, he cannot see the kingdom of God." (John 3:3) We must

be born again if we are to provoke divine intervention and supernatural help from God.

THE FEAR OF GOD

"Though a sinner do evil an hundred times, and his days be prolonged, yet surely I know that it shall be well with them that fear God, which fear before him: But it shall not be well with the wicked, neither shall he prolong his days, which are as a shadow; because he feareth not before God." (Eclessiastes 8:12-13) Unless we develop a healthy fear for God and His Kingdom, we will never experience the supernatural in life.

RIGHTEOUS LIFESTYLE

"And the work of righteousness shall be peace; and the effect of righteousness quietness and assurance forever." (Isaiah 32:17) Righteousness must become our lifestyle if we are to provoke divine intervention and emerge champions in life.

INTEGRITY

"The integrity of the upright shall guide them." (Proverbs 11:3)

AGREEMENT

"Can two walk together, except they be agreed?" (Amos 3:3)

"But if he will not hear thee, then take with thee one or two more, that in the mouth of two or three witnesses every word may be established. Verily I say unto you, Whatsoever ye shall bind on earth shall be bound in heaven: and whatsoever ye shall loose on earth shall be loosed in heaven. Again I say unto you, That if two of you shall agree on earth as touching any thing that they shall ask, it shall be done for them of my Father which is in heaven. For where two or three are gathered together in my name, there am I in the midst of them." (Matthew 18:16-20)

THE RIGHT WORDS

Job 6:25 declares, *"How forcible are right words! Jesus said there is no idle word in the kingdom. Every time you speak, your words are judged by the angels of the living God."*

"Suffer not thy mouth to cause thy flesh to sin; neither say thou before the angel, that it was an error: wherefore should God be angry at thy voice, and destroy the work of thine hands? The right

words will bring us out of captivity, the right word will provoke the Holy Spirit to come for your rescue." (Ecclesiastes 5:6"

SOUL WINNING

"And Jesus came and spake unto them, saying, All power is given unto me in heaven and in earth. Go ye therefore, and teach all nations, baptizing them in the name of the Father, and of the Son, and of the Holy Ghost: Teaching them to observe all things whatsoever I have commanded you: and, lo, I am with you always, even unto the end of the world. Amen." (Matthew 28:18-20)

OBEDIENCE

"In whom ye also trusted, after that ye heard the word of truth, the gospel of your salvation: in whom also after that ye believed, ye were sealed with that holy Spirit of promise." (Ephesians 1:13)

"Obey them that have the rule over you, and submit yourselves: for they watch for your souls, as they that must give account, that they may do it with joy, and not with grief: for that is unprofitable for you." (Hebrews 13:17)

PRAY IN THE SPIRIT

When you pray in the SPIRIT you are not speaking to men but unto GOD. *"For he that speaketh in an unknown tongue speaketh not unto men, but unto God: for no man understandeth him; howbeit in the spirit he speaketh mysteries."* (1 Corinthians 14:2)

CONCLUSION

As thou knowest not what is the way of the spirit, nor how the bones do grow in the womb of her that is with child: even so thou knowest not the works of God who maketh all.
Ecclesiastes 11:5

Unless we develop faith in God, we will never experience supernatural encounters. Unless we develop faith in God, we will never have access into **signs** and **wonders**. *"But without faith it is impossible to please him: for he that cometh to God must believe that he is, and that he is a rewarder of them that diligently seek him."* (Hebrews 11:6)

Let us hear the conclusion of the whole matter: Fear God, and keep his commandments: for this is the whole duty of man. For God shall bring every work into judgment, with every secret thing, whether it be good, or whether it be evil.
Ecclesiastes 12:13-14

Unless we repent from unrighteousness, we will forever live in frustration. The Bible says in Ecclesiastes 12:14—*"For God shall bring every work into judgment,"* with every secret thing, whether it be good, or whether it be evil. If you are a born again Christian, we'd like to encourage you in your Christian life. If you are not a born again Christian, we can help you here receive genuine salvation.

"Therefore if any man be in Christ, he is a new creature: old things are passed away; behold, all things are become new. Now repeat this Prayer after me." (2 Corinthians 5:17)

Say Lord Jesus, I accept you today, as my Lord and my savior. Forgive me of my sins, wash me with your blood. Right now, I believe, I am sanctified. I am saved, I am free. I am free from the power of sin to serve the Lord Jesus. Thank you, Lord, for saving me. Amen.

Congratulations.

YOU ARE NOW A BORN AGAIN CHRISTIAN!

AGAIN I SAY TO YOU CONGRATULATION

What must I do to determine my divine visitation?

To determine divine visitation you must be born again! The word says as many as received him, to them gave He power to become the sons of God. Even to them that believe on his name.

To qualify for divine visitation, do the following sincerely:

1) Acknowledge that you are a sinner and that He died for you. (Romans 3:23)

2) Repent of your sins. (Acts 3:19, Luke 13:5, 2 Peter 3:9)

3) Believe in your heart that Jesus died for your sin.(Romans 10:10)

4) Confess Jesus as the Lord over your life. (Romans 10:10, Acts 2:21)

NOW REPEAT THIS PRAYER AFTER ME:

Say Lord Jesus, I accept you today, as my Lord and my savior, forgive me of my sins wash me with your blood. Right now, I believe, I am sanctified, I am save, I am free, I am free from the Power of sin to serve the Lord Jesus. Thank you Lord for saving me. Amen.

Congratulations. You are now...

...a BORN AGAIN CHRISTIAN.

Again I say to you—CONGRATULATIONS!

I adjure you to watch the Spirit of God bear witness with your Spirit confirming His word with signs following. The word says The Spirit itself beareth witness with our spirit, that we are the children of God. Join a Bible-believing church or join us on our weekly and Sunday worship services at 343 Sanford Avenue Newark, New Jersey 07106.

Chapter 3   The Conquering Power of Healing

WISDOM KEYS

— Every productive society is a society heading to the top.

—Millions of Nigerians run away from Nigeria. Very few Nigerians stay in Nigeria.

—My decision to return Nigeria is the will of God for my life.

—My shortcoming in America after 18 years is the fact that I've trained me to be wise, to think, reflect and reason appropriately.

—If you train your mind to reason, it will train your hands to earn money.

—It is absurd to use the money of the heathen to build the kingdom of the living God.

—Every ministry reveals its agenda and VISION either at the beginning or at the end.

—Be careful of your life. It is your first ministry.

—The average American mind is conditioned

for a continual quest to get new things and discard the old.

—When I considered well, my BMW jeep became my initial deposit for the work of the ministry in Nigeria.

—Money will never fall from any tree or person. Make up your mind to be independent today.

—Everyone is waiting for you to change your mind. Until you change your thinking, nothing changes around you.

—Multiple academic degrees in other disciplines gave me the chance to think and reason.

—Whatever anyone is thinking at any time reveals what is inside of their heart.

—All planned events are the product of meditation.

—Every event is designed for a designated timeline.

Chapter 3 The Conquering Power of Healing

—Wisdom is your ability to think, to create and invent.

— If you can think wisely enough, you will come out of debt.

—The distance between you and your success is your innovative and creative ability to think well.

—Success is the result of hard work, commitment, resolve and determined learning from past mistakes and failings.

—If you organize your mind, you have organized your life and destiny.

—There is a thin line between success and failure.

—Wealth is your ability to think, power is your ability to reason and success is your ability to be informed.

—If you can make use of your mind by thinking and reasoning, God will make use of your life and destiny.

—Reflect, reason, think and be Great.

—Famous people are born of woman.

—That you will make it is your intention, that you will survive is your resolve, that you will succeed with changes is your determination, personal efforts and hard work.

—No man was born a failure.

—Lack of vision is the result of failure.

—Working with mental patients encourages and aspire me to be a productive observant and dedicated to my assignment.

—Successful people are not magicians. It is the willpower, combined with hard work and determination and a resolve to succeed, that make them succeed.

—In the unequivocal state of the mind, intention is not a location or a position. It is the state of the mind.

—So many people think that they think.

Chapter 3 The Conquering Power of Healing

—The mind is used to think, to reflect and to reason.

—You will remain blind with your eyes open until you can see with your mind by thinking.

—There is no favoritism in accurate and precise calculation.

—Although knowledge is power, information is the key and gateway to a great future.

—It will take the hand of God to move the hand of man.

—With the backing of the great wise God, nothing will disconnect you from your inheritance.

—As long as you have wisdom and understanding of God, Satan and evil cannot manipulate your life and destiny.

—You have come this far in life by your own judgment and the decisions you made in the past. Now lean in and listen to God for another dimension of greatness.

—Great people are ordinary people. It is extra ordinary efforts and the price of sacrifice that produces greatness in them.

—As a mental direct care worker, I saw a great pastor and a motivational speaker within myself.

—A menial job does not reduce your self-worth. Until you resolve to achieve greatness and see greatness in all you do, you will never count in your community.

—The principle of Jesus will solve your gambling and addiction problems.

—The man of Jesus will lead you into heaven.

—Everyone has their self-appraisal and what they think about you. Until you discover yourself, other opinions about you will alter the real you.

—Supervisors and directors are just a position in the chain of command in a workplace. Never allow your supervisor hierarchy to alter your opinion of yourself.

—Everyone can come out of debt if they make up their mind.

—The fact that I am not a decision-maker at work does not diminish my contribution to my world.

—Although it appears like it was a poor decision to accept a direct care employment at a psychiatric hospital, as I reflect on my nine years of that experience, it became apparent that I have learned and experienced enough for my next assignment.

—Self-encouragement and determination is a resolve of the heart.

—If you are determined to make a difference and do the things that make a difference, you will eventually make a difference.

—Good things do not come easy.

—Short cuts will cut your life short.

—Those who look ahead move ahead.

—Life is all about making an impact. In your lifetime strive to make an impact in your community.

—Make friends and connect with people who are moving ahead of you in life.

—If you can look around well, you have come a long way in your life, made a lot of difference and realized a lot of success in life.

—If you are my old friend, hurry up to reach out to me before I become a stranger to you.

—I am blessed with inspirations from God that changed my interpretation of the world around me.

—I thought I was stagnant and lonely until I looked around and noticed my children running around and my wife cooking.

— At 40, I resigned my job to seek the Lord forever.

—My ministry took a drastic rise to the top when the wisdom of God visited me with knowledge and understanding.

—You will be a better person if you understand the characteristics of your personality like your mood swings, attitudes and habits.

—It is the seed of love you sow into the heart of a child and a woman that you reap in due time.

—Love is not selfish. Love shares everything, including the concealed secrets of the mind.

—As long as you have a prayer life and a Bible, you will never feel lonely in the race of life.

—When good friends disconnect from you, let them go. They might have seen something new in a different direction.

—Confidence in yourself and in God is the only way to bring you out of captivity

—Never train a child to waste his or her time.

—The mind is the greatest asset of a great future.

—You walk by common sense, run by principles and fly by instruction.

—Those who become successful in life did it by self-determination, hard work and learning from past failures.

—Most successful people are lonely people. No one renders help to them, believing they are already successful. Except when they seek for more knowledge and information, they are all alone.

— I have seen a towing truck vehicle. I have also seen a towing ship in the water. But I have never seen a towing airplane in the air.

—I exercise my judgment and make a decision every minute of the day. Decisions are crucial, critical and vital with reference to your future.

—So many people wish for a great future. You can only work towards a great future.

—Your celebrity status began when you discovered your talent. What are you good at? Work at it with all your commitment.

—Prayers will sustain you, but the wisdom of God will prosper you.

—When I met Oyedepo, his teachings changed my perspective. But when I met Ibiyeomie, his teachings changed my perception.

— I will be successful in ministry if only I concentrate and focus my energy in the work of the ministry.

— It took the late Dr. Norman Vincent Peale's book to open my mind towards the kingdom of success.

CHAPTER 4

PRAYER OF SALVATION

Neither is there salvation in any other: for there is none other name under heaven given among men, whereby we must be saved.
Acts 4:12

My question to you here is: are you saved?

You are not safe until you are saved. Heaven and hell is real. Where do you plan to spend eternity? In heaven, at last, with God and His angels? Or in hell fire?

What must I do to be saved?

The jailer asked, *"What must I do to be saved? And they said, Believe on the Lord Jesus Christ, and thou shalt be saved, and thy house."* (Acts 16:30-31)

To determine divine visitation you must be born again! The word says as many as received him, to them gave He power to become the sons of God. Even to them that believe on his name.

To qualify for divine visitation, do the following sincerely:

1) Acknowledge that you are a sinner and that He died for you. (Romans 3:23)

2) Repent of your sins. (Acts 3:19, Luke 13:5, 2 Peter 3:9)

3) Believe in your heart that Jesus died for your sin.(Romans 10:10)

4) Confess Jesus as the Lord over your life. (Romans 10:10, Acts 2:21)

NOW REPEAT THIS PRAYER AFTER ME:

Say Lord Jesus, I accept you today, as my Lord and my savior, forgive me of my sins wash me with your blood. Right now, I believe, I am sanctified, I am save, I am free, I am free from the Power of sin to serve the Lord Jesus. Thank you Lord for saving me. Amen.

Congratulations. You are now...

...a BORN AGAIN CHRISTIAN.

Again I say to you—CONGRATULATIONS!

I adjure you to watch the Spirit of God bear witness with your Spirit confirming His word with signs following. The word says The Spirit itself beareth witness with our spirit, that we are the children of God.

MIRACLE CARE OUTREACH

"...But that the members should have the same care one for another"
1 Corinthians 12:25

We are all members of the body of Christ. Jesus commanded us to love our neighbor as ourselves. This includes caring for one another as a member of one body. True love is expressed in caring and giving. The word says, for God so Love He gave....

Reach out to someone in need of Jesus. Help someone in crisis find Christ. Look out and prove your love to Jesus by caring and inviting your friends and associates to find Jesus the Healer.

Invite your friends to our Home Care Cell Fellowship (Miracle Chapel Intl. Satellite Fellowship). We're in the U.S. at 33 Schley Street, Newark, New Jersey 07112. Home Care Cell Fellowship Group meets every Tuesday at 6:00pm-7:00pm.

If you are in Nigeria—MIRACLE OF GOD MINISTRIES, aka "MIRACLE CHAPEL INTL." Mpama–Egbu-Owerri Imo state Nigeria.

LIFE IS NOT ALL ABOUT DURATION, BUT IT'S ALL ABOUT DONATION

What does this statement mean?

Life consists not in accumulation of material wealth. (Luke 12:15) But it's all about liberality…i.e., what you can give and share with others. (Proverbs 11:25) When you live for others, you live forever—because you outlive your generation by the legacy you leave behind after you depart into glory to be with the Lord. But when you live for yourself, when you are reduced to SELF—you are easily forgotten when you die and depart in glory.

Permit me to admonish you today to live your life to be a blessing to a soul connected to you today. I want you to know that so many souls are connected and looking up to you, and through you so many souls will be saved and rescued from destruction. Will you disciple someone today to find Jesus Christ?

As a genuine Christian, it is your duty to evangelize Jesus Christ to all you meet on your way. Jesus is still in the healing business—Jesus is still doing miracles, from time of old to now. Therefore, tell someone about Jesus Christ today, disciple and bring them to Church. *Philip findeth Nathanael...* (John 1:45)

Please prove the sincerity of your love for God today, please become a soul winner. The dignity of your Christianity is hidden in your boldness to proclaim and evangelize Jesus Christ to all you meet on your way. There is a question mark on the integrity of your Christianity until you become a life soul winner. Invite someone to join us worship the Lord Jesus this coming Sunday. Amen.

Chapter 4   Prayer of Salvation

MIRACLE OF GOD MINISTRIES

PILLARS OF THE COMMISSION

We Believe, Preach and Practice the following:

1) We believe and preach Salvation to every living human being.

2) We believe and preach Repentance and Forgiveness of sins.

3) We believe and preach the baptism of the Holy Spirit and Spiritual gifts.

4) We believe and teach Prosperity.

5) We believe and preach Divine Healing and Miracles—Signs and Wonder.

6) We believe and preach Faith.

7) We believe and proclaim the Power of God (Supernatural).

8) We believe and proclaim Praise and Worship to God.

9) We believe and preach Wisdom.

10) We believe and preach Holiness (Consecration).

11) We believe and preach Vision.

12) We believe and teach the Word of God.

13) We believe and teach Success.

14) We believe and practice Prayer.

15) We believe and teach Deliverance.

These 15 stones form the Pillars of Our Commission. Become part of this church family and follow this great move of God.

Chapter 4   Prayer of Salvation

MY HEARTFELT PRAYER FOR YOU

A greater portion of our ministry is to see you encounter God. I desire to hear testimonies of what the Lord is doing in our individual lives. The reason we create books, brochures, magazines, mp3s, DVDs and audio tapes is to have available material that will help boast your faith in God. Please take advantage of any of our resource materials that come your way. There is something God has in stock for us that we must discover.

We do not debate about doctrines, philosophy or logic. We are all about proving the immutability of the power of God, through His undiluted word—the Bible. I guarantee most of our ministry material is designed to build your faith and spiritual life.

Now let me pray for you:

Heavenly father, I come to you today seeking your timely intervention into the life of the precious friend reading this book. May they encounter your power in a supernatural dimension that is inexplicable to man's understanding. Lord, grant them the desires of their heart and give them a genuine reason to know you more. I thank you, Jesus, because you are still in the healing business. Even now, I pray that you will heal this precious soul from the top of his/her head, to the soles of his/her feet. Thank you, Jesus, for hearing me. In Jesus's mighty name, I have prayed. Amen.

INEXPLICABLE FAITH

Inexplicable faith is the faith that cannot be seen, yet cannot be denied. Putting our faith in line is all it takes for God to move in our direction. Those great things happening in our lives that we cannot explain how they came about—that is the summary of this small book. *"This is the Lord's doing; it is marvellous in our eyes."* (Psalms 118:23)

A few years ago, God moved in an unquestionable dimension in my life that I could not deny—yet I couldn't explain it. May you experience God as you put away this book today, in the mighty name of Jesus. Amen. I pray that God surprises you with supernatural happenings in your life, that all around you cannot deny—yet you cannot explain it.

Chapter 4   Prayer of Salvation

WE MUST ACKNOWLEDGE THE LORD, OUR GOD

"Because they regard not the works of the Lord, nor the operation of his hands, he shall destroy them, and not build them up." (Pslams 28:5)

As believers, we must acknowledge the hand of the Lord in our lives. Every time we deny His acts in our lives, we provoke supernatural destruction upon our world. As you read this book, we'd like you to take time out of your busy schedule and recognize all the good things that God has done in your life.

WE MUST REMEMBER THE LORD, OUR GOD

"But thou shalt remember the Lord thy God: for it is he that giveth thee power to get wealth, that he may establish his covenant which he sware unto thy fathers, as it is this day." (Deuteronomy 8:18)

It is divine not to forget the Lord. We must always be conscious of the doings of the Lord God in our respective lives.

"Then beware lest thou forget the Lord, which brought thee forth out of the land of Egypt,

from the house of bondage." (Deuteronomy 6:12)

WE MUST FOREVER GIVE THANKS UNTO THE LORD

O give thanks unto the Lord; for he is good:
for his mercy endureth for ever.
O give thanks unto the God of gods:
for his mercy endureth for ever.
O give thanks to the Lord of lords:
for his mercy endureth for ever.
Psalms 136:1-3

During Thanksgiving we recognize the goodness of the Lord in our lives. The holy scriptures teaches and admonishes us to constantly give thanks to God, for continual promotion, breakthrough and success in life.

CHAPTER 5
ABOUT THE AUTHOR

Rev. Franklin N. Abazie is the founding and Presiding Pastor of Miracle of God Ministries, with headquarters in Newark, New Jersey USA and a branch church in Owerri-Imo State Nigeria. He is following the footsteps of one of his mentors, the healing evangelist Oral Roberts of the blessed memory. The Lord passed Oral Roberts' healing mantle two days before he went to be with the Lord at age 91 into the hands of healing evangelist Rev. Franklin N. Abazie in a vision.

In all his services, the Power and Presence of God is present to heal all in his audience. Rev. Abazie is an ordained man of God, with a Healing Ministry reviving the healing and miracle ministry of Jesus Christ of Nazareth.

Pastor Franklin N. Abazie, has been called by God with a unique mandate: **"THE MOMENT IS DUE TO IMPACT YOUR WORLD THROUGH THE REVIVAL OF THE HEALING AND MIRACLE MINIS-**

TRY OF JESUS CHRIST OF NAZARETH.

"I AM SENDING YOU TO RESTORE HEALTH UNTO THEE AND I WILL HEAL THEE OF THY WOUNDS, SAID THE LORD OF HOST."

Rev. Abazie is a gifted, ardent teacher of the word of God, who operates also in the office of a Prophet, generating and attracting undeniable signs and wonders, special miracles and healings, with apostolic fireworks of the Holy Ghost. He is the founding and presiding senior Pastor of this fast growing Healing Ministry. He has written over 86 inspirational, healing and transforming books covering almost all aspects of divine healing and life. He is happily married and blessed with children.

Chapter 5   About the Author

BOOKS BY REV. FRANKLIN N. ABAZIE:

1) *The Outcome of Faith*
2) *Understanding the Secret of Prevailing Prayers*
3) *Commanding Abundance*
4) *Understanding the Secret of the Man God Uses*
5) *Activating My Due Season*
6) *Overcoming Divine Verdicts*
7) *The Outcome of Divine Wisdom*
8) *Understanding God's Restoration Mandate*
9) *Walking In the Victory and Authority of the Truth*
10) *God's Covenant Exemption*
11) *Destiny Restoration Pillars*
12) *Provoking Acceptable Praise*
13) *Understanding Divine Judgment*
14) *Activating Angelic Re-enforcement*
15) *Provoking Un-Merited Favo*
16) *The Benefits of the Speaking Faith*
17) *Understanding Divine Arrangement*
18) *How to Keep Your Healing*
19) *Understanding the Mysteries of the Speaking Faith*
20) *Understanding the Mysteries of Prophetic Healing*
21) *Operating Under the Rules of Creative Healing*
22) *Understanding the Joy of Breakthrough*
23) *Understanding the Mystery of Breakthrough*
24) *Understanding Divine Prosperity*
25) *Understanding Divine Healing*

26) Retaining Your Inheritance
27) Overcoming Confusing Spirit
28) Commanding Angelic Escorts
29) Enforcing Your Inheritance In Christ Jesus
30) Understanding Your Guardian Angels
31) Overcoming the Dominion of Sin
32) Understanding the Voice of God
33) The Outstanding Benefits of the Anointing
34) The Audacity of the Blood of Jesus
35) Walking in the Reality of the Anointing
36) Escaping the Nightmare of Poverty
37) Understanding Your Harvest Season
38) Activating Your Success Buttons
39) Overcoming the Forces of Darkness
40) Overcoming the Devices of the Devil
41) Overcoming Demonic Agents
42) Overcoming the Sorrows of Failure
43) Rejecting the Sorrows of Failure
44) Resisting the Sorrows of Poverty
45) Restoring Broken Marriages
46) Redeeming Your Days
47) The Force of Vision
48) Overcoming the Forces of Ignorance
49) Understanding the Sacrifice of Small Beginning
50) The Might of Small Beginning
51) Understanding the Mysteries of Prophesy
52) Overcoming Dream Nightmares

53) Breaking the Shackles of the Curse of the Law
54) Understanding the Joy of Harvest
55) Wisdom for Signs & Wonders
56) Wisdom for Generational Impact
57) Wisdom for Marriage Stability
58) Understanding the Number of Your Days
59) Enforcing Your Kingdom Rights
60) Escaping the Traps of Immoralities
61) Escaping the Trap of Poverty
62) Accessing Biblical Prosperity
63) Accessing True Riches in Christ
64) Silencing the Voice of the Accuser
65) Overcoming the Forces of Oppositions
66) Quenching the Voice of the Avenger
67) Silencing Demonic Prediction & Projection
68) Silencing Your Mocker
69) Understanding the Power of the Holy Ghost
70) Understanding the Baptism of Power
71) The Mystery of the Blood of Jesus
72) Understanding the Mystery of Sanctification
73) Understanding the Power of Holiness
74) Understanding the Forces of Purity & Righteousness
75) Activating the Forces of Vengeance
76) Appreciating the Mystery of Restoration
77) Overcoming the Projection & Prediction of the Enemy
78) Engaging the Mystery of the Blood
79) Commanding the Power of the Speaking Faith

80) Uprooting the Forces Against Your Rising
81) Overcoming Mere Success Syndrome
82) Understanding Divine Sentence
83) Understanding the Mystery of Praise
84) Understanding the Author of Faith
85) The Mystery of the Finisher of Faith
86) Attracting Supernatural Favor

MIRACLE OF GOD MINISTRIES

NIGERIA CRUSADE 2012

MIRACLE OF GOD MINISTRIES
NIGERIA CRUSADE
2012

MIRACLE OF GOD MINISTRIES
NIGERIA CRUSADE 2012

MIRACLE OF GOD MINISTRIES

NIGERIA CRUSADE

2012

MIRACLE OF GOD MINISTRIES

NIGERIA CRUSADE

2012

www.ingramcontent.com/pod-product-compliance
Lightning Source LLC
Chambersburg PA
CBHW031158020426
42333CB00013B/726